C000154960

13087

Autumn

LABURNUM PRESS

Stephen White-Thomson

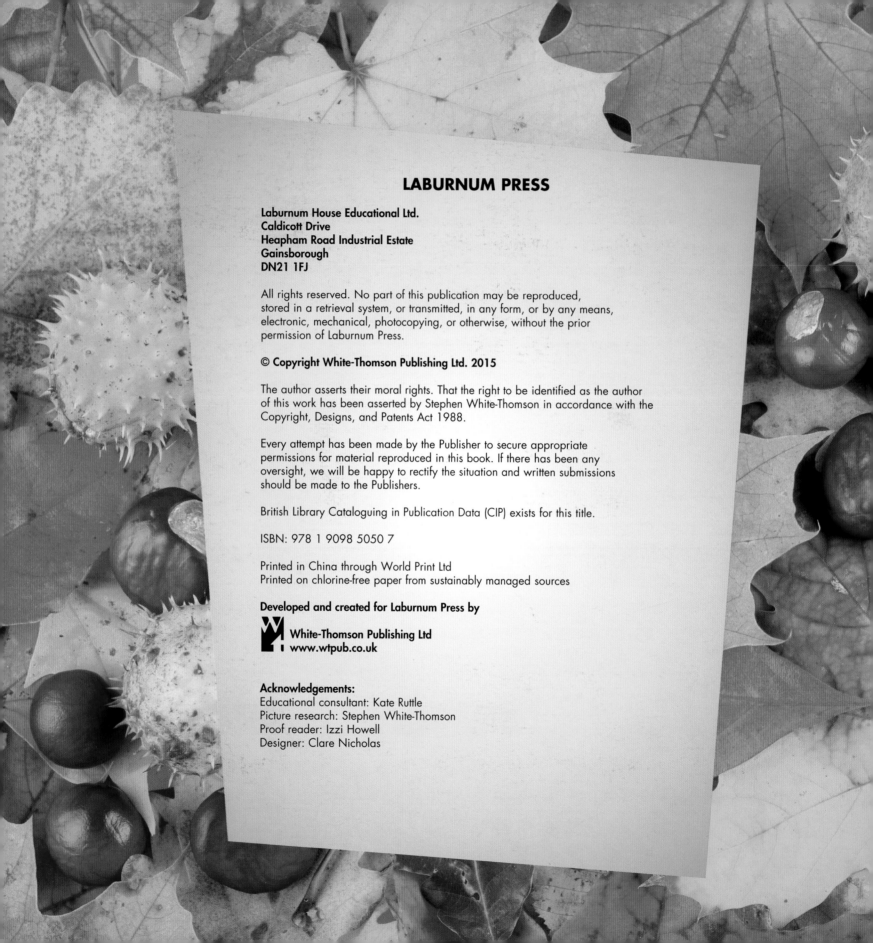

LABURNUM PRESS

Laburnum House Educational Ltd.
Caldicott Drive
Heapham Road Industrial Estate
Gainsborough
DN21 1FJ

British Library Cataloguing in Publication Data (CIP) exists for this title.

ISBN: 978 1 9098 5050 7

Printed in China through World Print Ltd
Printed on chlorine-free paper from sustainably managed sources

Developed and created for Laburnum Press by

White-Thomson Publishing Ltd
www.wtpub.co.uk

Acknowledgements:
Educational consultant: Kate Ruttle
Picture research: Stephen White-Thomson
Proof reader: Izzi Howell
Designer: Clare Nicholas

Contents

Autumn Weather

In autumn, the weather becomes cooler and wetter.

hat

scarf

gloves

4

What do you need to wear when it rains hard?

Changing colours

This is a tree in summer.

This is a tree in autumn.

What's happened to the leaves?

Autumn leaves

In America, autumn is called fall.

Why do you think autumn is called fall?

9

Autumn harvest

Apples become ripe

in autumn.

You can pick

them off trees.

Stretch!

10

Can you name some of these harvest fruit and vegetables?

Autumn celebrations

What do you do when it's Halloween?

pumpkin

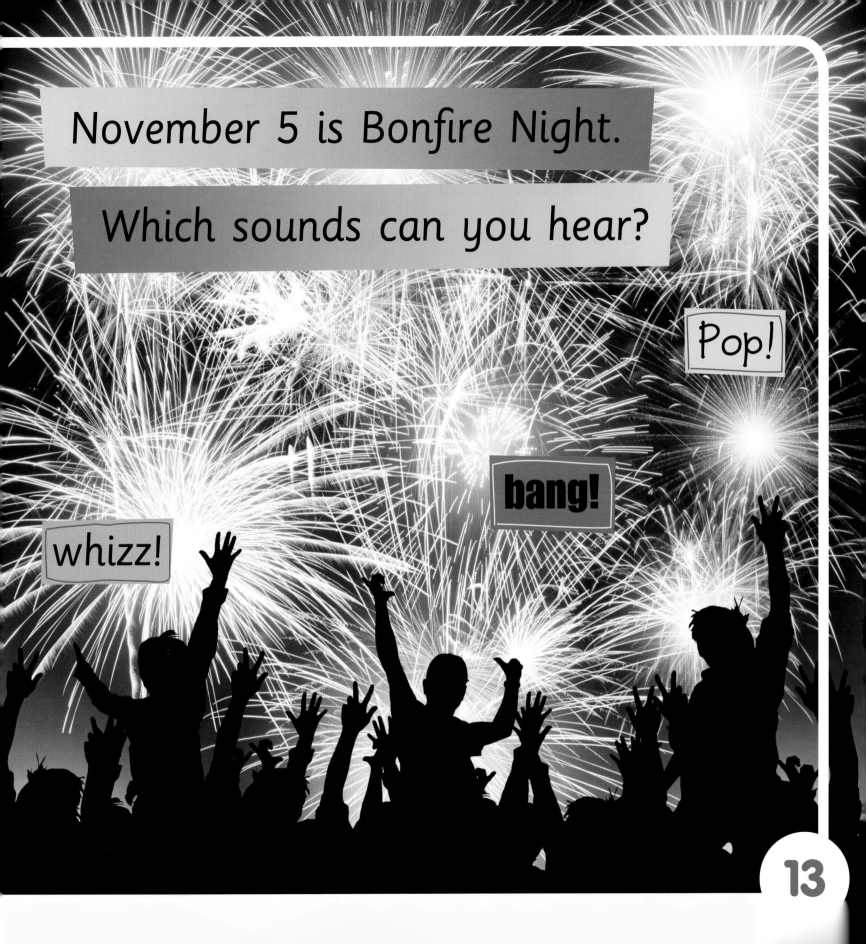

Autumn festivals

The Hindu festival of Divali is celebrated in autumn.

diva

rangoli

Jewish people eat apples and honey to celebrate Rosh Hashanah.

15

On the farm

Tractors plough the fields.

Farmers plant seeds.

Cows are moved into cowsheds to keep warm.

Autumn seeds

Which trees do these

seeds grow into?

acorn

prickly

shiny

These conkers grow on

horse-chestnut trees.

Autumn animals

Hedgehogs eat lots of food before they hibernate in winter.

In autumn, squirrels bury nuts.

They dig them up during the winter.

Notes for adults

Sparklers books are designed to support and extend the learning of young children. Regular winners of Practical Pre-School silver and gold awards, the books' high-interest subjects link to the Early Years curriculum and beyond. Find out more about Early Years foundation stages (EYFS) at www.gov.uk/government/publications/early-years-foundation-stage-framework–2, and reading with children from the National Literacy Trust (www.literacytrust.org.uk).

Themed titles
Autumn is one of four **Seasons** titles that encourage children to learn about the fun and informative aspects of their lives in the different seasons. The other titles are **Winter** (ISBN: 978 1 9098 5051 4), **Spring** (ISBN: 978 1 9098 5048 4) and **Summer** (ISBN: 978 1 9098 5049 1)

The prime areas of learning: (taught in nurseries)
- communication and language
- physical development
- personal, social and emotional development

The specific areas of learning: (taught in reception classes)
- literacy
- mathematics
- understanding the world
- expressive arts and design

Making the most of reading time
When reading with younger children, take time to explore the pictures together. Ask children to find, identify and count or describe different objects. Point out colours and textures. Allow quiet spaces in your reading so that children can ask questions or repeat your words. Try pausing mid-sentence so that children can predict the next word. This sort of participation develops early reading skills.

Follow the words with your finger as you read. The main text is in Infant Sassoon, a clear, friendly font designed for children learning to read and write. The label and sound effects add fun and give the opportunity to distinguish between levels of communication. Where appropriate, labels, sound effects or main text may be presented phonetically. Encourage children to imitate the sounds.

As you read the book, you can also take the opportunity to talk about the book itself with appropriate vocabulary such as "page", "cover", "back", "front", "label" and "page number".

You can also extend children's learning by using the books as a springboard for discussion and further activities. There are a few suggestions on the facing page.

Pages 4–5
From the end of summer, keep a doll or teddy to dress each day during autumn. What will it need to wear? At the beginning, it might need a jumper instead of a t-shirt and tights or trousers instead of shorts. Think about outdoor clothes: Coat? Boots? Hat? Scarf? Umbrella? Talk about why it needs each of these items of clothing. Help children to link clothing to weather.

Pages 5–6
Look at live webcam feeds from the countryside and photographs of autumn colours. Help the children to make wool-windings. Each child will need a playing-card-sized piece of cardboard. Place parallel strips of double-sided tape lengthways on the cardboard. Ask children to look carefully at the colours they can see and match to wool of each colour. They should wind the wool carefully around the cardboard.

Pages 8–9
If you have easy access to outside areas, take the children out to play with the leaves. Listen as you crunch them underfoot. Help the children to gather some of the leaves. Use them to make leaf prints in autumnal colours.

Pages 10–11
Make a fruit salad from autumn fruits: apples, blackberries, plums, pears. Let the children help you to prepare the salad while you talk about the size, colour, seeds and stalks of each fruit. Make a pictogram showing who liked which of the fruits.

Pages 12–13
Use different styles of artwork to make firework pictures. Try splatter painting, or using straws to blow paint across black paper. Try dipping string into paint for printing Catherine wheels, or using the sides of lollipop sticks or waxresist or chalk pastels. Display your paintings with signs showing firework sound effects.

Pages 14–15
Go online and show children images of Rangoli patterns. Make or download a simple template and help them to use coloured sand or glitter to fill each section (you can either glue the section to create patterns to keep, or accept that your sand/glitter will be mixed when you reuse it).

Pages 16–17
Fill trays with soil. Make the soil in some of the trays damp and keep other trays dry. Give children forks to drag through the soil like a plough. Ask children to observe what happens when they pull their fork through the different soils. Introduce the song 'Oats and Beans and Barley Grow' (words and animations are easily available online).

Pages 18–19
Check whether children are allergic to nuts. If they are, do this activity outside. Gather a selection of nuts either from the woods (e.g. acorn, hazelnut, cobnut, conker) or unshelled nuts from the supermarket. Let children handle the nuts and think of words to describe them. Then put them in order of size, prickliness and depth of colour.

Page 20–21
Visit websites such as BBC's AutumnWatch to see how different animals behave in the winter. Make a class book with photographs, children's pictures and simple sentences about each of the animals you see. Encourage the children to read the book. Gradually, add more text in the form of labels and captions.

Index

Picture acknowledgements:
iStock: 11 (MagMos); **Shutterstock**: 4 (Sergey Novikov), 6 (Roman Samokhin), 7 (Artens); **Thinkstock**: cover (ulkas), 5 (Stockbyte), 8-9 (SerrNovik), 10 (fotostic), 12 (Comstock), 13 (iprostocks), 14 (soumenNath), 15 (ddsign_stock), 16 (fotokostic), 17 (Sponner), 18 (sereznly)cover (ulkas), 19 (iStock), 20 (Przemyslaw Rzeszutko), 21 (Fireglo2). Background to 2, 3, 22, 23, 24 Shutterstock/ballounm.